SAINT MARGARET OF CORTONA NOVENA

POWERFUL PRAYERS AND DEVOTIONS

FR EDMOND HART

Introduction

Italy was home to St. Margaret of Cortona throughout the 1200s. She had lived a wicked life and was now penitent. In the end, she decided to become a member of the Third Order of St. Francis and lead a life of penance.

Despite her history, St. Margaret of Cortona rose to become a truly pious woman. This novena is a great way to ask this contrite saint for help in your life!

Concerning Saint Margaret of Cortona

In the year 1247, St. Margaret of Cortona was born in Laviano, a tiny village in Italy. Margaret experienced her mother's death at the age of seven. Margaret's father remarried soon after. Margaret's new stepmother did not think highly of her, and the two did not get along.

Margaret became exceedingly obstinate during her adolescent years. She became known for her recklessness. She decided to flee with a nobleman she met when she was seventeen years old.

Rather than marrying Margaret, the nobleman made her his mistress and put her in his castle. She spent ten years living with this gentleman. They had a single son together.

During a journey, the nobleman once failed to return at the scheduled hour. Margaret fretted much when his dog arrived home without him. She found her lover's lifeless body in the forest after following the dog's lead. She witnessed his murder.

Margaret was deeply upset by her lover's murder. She decided to leave the nobleman's house after having regrets about her way of life. Margaret attempted to go back to her father's house, bringing her son along. But Margaret's stepmother refused to let her live with them.

Margaret then proceeded to the Franciscan friars in Cortona with her son. She led a life of penance there. She committed herself to prayer and fasted on bread and vegetables. Margaret finally became a member of the Third Order of St. Francis, and her son went on to become a friar as well. She immediately made progress in her spiritual life of prayer.

Margaret became devoted to Jesus' Passion and the Eucharist, and these devotions fostered her growth in charity. She begged for food and gave it to the needy, following in the footsteps of St. Francis of Assisi. She also founded a hospital for the underprivileged. To staff this hospital with nurses, she also organized a group of Third Order sisters.

She later founded a group of people to help the hospital and the less fortunate.

This order's members had a strong devotion to Our Lady of Mercy.

Furthermore, Margaret confronted her bishop, who was leading a very materialistic life and fought to implement much-needed reform in the Church.

In 1297, Margaret passed away. It was discovered that her body was uncorrupted after four centuries. Pope Benedict XIII declared her to be a saint in 1728.

The St. Margaret of Cortona Novena: Why Pray?

The patron saint of lone moms is St. Margaret of Cortona. If you are a single mother, you can ask for her help. Additionally, you might ask her to offer up prayers for a single mother you know.

The patroness of mental illness and mentally sick individuals is St. Margaret of Cortona. If you or someone you know is experiencing mental illness, you can pray this novena.

Furthermore, the patron saint of those who resist sexual temptation is St. Margaret of Cortona. If you or someone you know is experiencing sexual temptation, you can ask her to pray for them. Alternatively, you can ask her to pray for you if you're having trouble resisting these temptations.

Day 1 of St. Margaret of Cortona Novena

In the name of the Holy Spirit, the Father, and the Son.

Amen.

We are grateful that You provided us with St. Margaret of Cortona as a model of holiness, Dear Lord. Please enable us to follow her example of

repentance and conversion in our own lives.

St. Margaret, you endured suffering as a kid because your mother passed away when you were little. Although you had a very terrible childhood, you eventually chose to turn from your sin and follow God.

Kindly present my requests to God, the One you have chosen to serve!

You endured numerous hardships even though it was difficult for you to change your ways and become pious.

Please pray for me so that I might live a life that is worthy of serving God. Please pray for me so that I may never let adversity or hardship prevent me from being holy.

And in this novena, I specifically ask for (state your goals here).

Pray for us, St. Margaret of Cortona!

Through the power of the Holy Spirit, the Father, and the Son, amen.

Day 2 of St. Margaret of Cortona Novena

In the name of the Holy Spirit, the Father, and the Son.

Amen.

We are grateful that You provided us with St. Margaret of Cortona as a model of holiness, Dear Lord. Please enable us to follow her example of

repentance and conversion in our own lives.

St. Margaret, you had a very challenging early family life. You chose to live in sin apart from your family in part because of the death of your mother and the lack of love you received from your stepmother. However, you conquered this sinful life and gave your all to God.

Please present my requests to God, whom you so devotedly adored!

You were the parent of an unmarried child. You were able to raise your son in the faith despite your transgressions and hardships.

Please offer up prayers for me so that I can always heed God's call to serve Him. Please pray for me to be able to keep going after holiness despite whatever obstacles I may encounter.

And in this novena, I specifically ask for (state your goals here).

Pray for us, St. Margaret of Cortona!

In the name of the Holy Spirit, the Father, and the Son.

Amen.

Day 3 of St. Margaret of Cortona Novena

In the name of the Holy Spirit, the Father, and the Son.

Amen

We are grateful that You provided us with St. Margaret of Cortona as a model of holiness, Dear Lord. Please enable us to follow her example of

repentance and conversion in our own lives.

When you were a young woman, St. Margaret, you fled your family's abusive home. You had a child with a nobleman you decided to live with, even though he refused to marry you. You decided to turn from your sinful way of living and pursue purity.

Kindly present my requests to God, the One you have chosen to serve!

Your lover's murder made you aware of the errors in your life. You quickly started living a more moral life when you felt regret.

Please pray for me so that I won't ever grow accustomed to my shortcomings.

Please pray that I might make holiness my daily goal.

And in this novena, I specifically ask for (state your goals here).

Pray for us, St. Margaret of Cortona!

Through the power of the Holy Spirit, the Father, and the Son, amen.

Day 4 of the St. Margaret of Cortona Novena

In the name of the Holy Spirit, the Father, and the Son.

Amen.

We are grateful that You provided us with St. Margaret of Cortona as a model of holiness, Dear Lord. Please enable us to follow her example of

repentance and conversion in our own lives.

Saint Margaret, your lover's murder served as a wake-up call to your mistakes. You decided to give your life to God and turned from your immoral way of living. For the remainder of your life, you lived as a chaste and pure woman.

Kindly never stop presenting my requests before God's throne!

Following your conversion, you lead a life full of charitable deeds and acts of penitence. You dedicated many years to the search for holiness.

Please pray for me so that I can maintain all of my holiness-related resolutions. Please pray for me to be able to keep trying to serve God every day of my life.

And in this novena, I specifically ask for (state your goals here).

Pray for us, St. Margaret of Cortona!

In the name of the Holy Spirit, the Father, and the Son.

Amen.

Day 5 St. Margaret of Cortona Novena

In the name of the Holy Spirit, the Father, and the Son.

Amen.

We are grateful that You provided us with St. Margaret of Cortona as a model of holiness, Dear Lord. Please enable us to follow her example of

repentance and conversion in our own lives.

St. Margaret, in your early years, you decided to live as a man's mistress. However, you turned from your misdeeds and chose to pursue virtue out of love for God after your partner was murdered.

Kindly present my requests to God, the One you loved!

You made a difficult decision to live a life of holiness and penance. However, you remained steadfast in your resolve to turn your life around.

Please intercede for me so that I may work to develop all the virtues required for holiness. Please pray for me to become more devoted every day of my life.

And in this novena, I specifically ask for (state your goals here).

Pray for us, St. Margaret of Cortona!

Through the power of the Holy Spirit, the Father, and the Son, amen.

Day 6 St. Margaret of Cortona Novena

In the name of the Holy Spirit, the Father, and the Son.

Amen.

We are grateful that You provided us with St. Margaret of Cortona as a model of holiness, Dear Lord. Please enable us to follow her example of

repentance and conversion in our own lives.

Saint Margaret, following the assassination of your sweetheart, you decided to turn your life around. When you attempted to go back to your father's house, your stepmother would not accept you into their house and would not forgive you. Despite this mistreatment, you persisted in your pursuit of purity.

Please do not give up on presenting my requests before God's throne!

You gave yourself over to a life of fasting and repentance. You achieved remarkable sanctity despite your past.

Please pray for me so that I won't let my past transgressions or injuries stop me from pursuing holiness. Please pray for me to maintain my faith in the face of adversity.

And in this novena, I specifically ask for (state your goals here).

Pray for us, St. Margaret of Cortona!

In the name of the Holy Spirit, the Father, and the Son.

Amen.

Day 7 of St. Margaret of Cortona Novena

In the name of the Holy Spirit, the Father, and the Son.

Amen.

We are grateful that You provided us with St. Margaret of Cortona as a model of holiness, Dear Lord. Please enable us to follow her example of

repentance and conversion in our own lives.

After the assassination of your lover, St. Margaret, you decided to give up your previous life of sin. Your father and stepmother's house did not feel like a place for you to be. As a result of the welcoming of certain Franciscan friars, you were able to fully commit to a life of holy service.

Kindly present my requests to God, the One you have chosen to serve!

You committed penance and charitable deeds for the remainder of your life. Even though you suffered and sinned in the past, you attained enormous sanctity.

Please pray for me so that I won't let anything stop me from pursuing virtue. Please pray for me to love God more and more every day.

And in this novena, I specifically ask for (state your goals here).

Pray for us, St. Margaret of Cortona! Through the power of the Holy Spirit, the Father, and the Son, amen.

Day 8 St. Margaret of Cortona Novena

In the name of the Holy Spirit, the Father, and the Son.

Amen.

We are grateful that You provided us with St. Margaret of Cortona as a model of holiness, Dear Lord. Please enable us to follow her example of

repentance and conversion in our own lives.

St. Margaret, when your father and stepmother would not let you stay in their house, you took refuge with a community of Franciscan friars. You committed yourself to acts of holy service in your new life of penitence out of love for God.

Please don't stop presenting my requests to God, the One you loved so much!

By giving to the needy and begging for food, you emulated St. Francis of Assisi. You accomplished so much good as you provided treatment for the impoverished by establishing a hospital for them.

Please intercede for me so that I may always seize the chance to glorify God by helping my neighbour. Pray for me to be able to respond to God's call to serve Him in whatever manner He sees fit.

And in this novena, I specifically ask for (state your goals here).

Pray for us, St. Margaret of Cortona!

In the name of the Holy Spirit, the Father, and the Son.

Amen.

Day 9 St. Margaret of Cortona Novena

In the name of the Holy Spirit, the Father, and the Son.

Amen.

We are grateful that You provided us with St. Margaret of Cortona as a model of holiness, Dear Lord. Please enable us to follow her example of

repentance and conversion in our own lives.

Dear St. Margaret of Cortona, you decided to give up your sinful life and dedicate yourself fully to serving God as a Third Order Franciscan. You committed the rest of your life to serving God.

Please present my requests to God, Whom you so devotedly served!

Serving the Church was something you did in addition to performing deeds of penance and charity. You stood up to your secular bishop and made every effort to help him become a more holy person.

Please intercede for me so that I will always be willing to serve God and His Church. Please pray for me so that my devotion to God will never fade.

And in this novena, I specifically ask for (state your goals here).

Pray for us, St. Margaret of Cortona!

In the name of the Holy Spirit, the Father, and the Son.

Amen.

Made in the USA
Las Vegas, NV
02 March 2024

86629589R00022